I0105617

VISION

Going To The Next Level

A PROGRAM BY VIRGIL C. REVISH

Copyright © 2025 Virgil C. Revish.

All rights reserved. No part of this book may be reproduced, stored,
or transmitted by any means—whether auditory, graphic, mechanical, or
electronic—without written permission of both publisher
and author, except in the case of brief excerpts used in critical articles and
reviews. Unauthorized reproduction of any part of this
work is illegal and is punishable by law.

ISBN: 978-1-963917-95-6 (paperback)
ISBN: 978-1-963917-96-3 (hardcover)
ISBN: 978-1-966954-00-2(ebook)

Library of Congress Control Number:2025903260

CONTENTS

Proverbs 29:18
King James Version (KJV)
18 Where there is no vision, the people perish…

What is VISION?

Generally speaking, VISION is the ability to see, even in your imagination and/or in your future. It is "a picture in your mind."

My vision is to provide a resource document that will help individuals set their goals and take constructive steps to achieve them.

Each vision is different. Each path bears its own challenges. The accomplishment of any vision requires the individual to take definite steps toward meeting certain goals.

VISION is what you can see….what you can achieve. I invite you to join your vision with mine so that you might grow, develop, achieve and succeed.

Your success will always start with your VISION.

Thank God for the favor He has bestowed on me and my life. I want to thank Him for purpose and for Vision. As He has blessed me, I hope that this publication will bless YOU.

INTRODUCTION

In all phases and stages of life, there are many options, opportunities, and paths that one can take. Usually, however, there is a process, that may have many roads that will lead an individual to success.

The purpose of this Manual is to identify and define some of the roads, opportunities, and options and to help the reader, through a planned program, to reach his/her destiny.

Without regard for the individual, everyone seeking success needs a VISION and a plan. This manual, *VISION – Going to the Next Level* is more than a plan. It is a program designed to help the reader/student hone the vision, create, improve, and execute the academic plan and necessary steps that take the Vision from a simple longing and desire to reality.

Let's get started now to define your Vision and understand as you prepare to take the steps that will lead to your success.

Setting your goals, doing your research, and taking the necessary steps are always important.

Best wishes to you as you begin your journey into your academic future.

– Virgil Revish
November, 2013

WHAT THIS MANUAL
IS NOT

This is just a manual designed to open your mind to some ideas you, parents, and students, may not have considered. It is just a guide. It does not attempt to present everything that anyone should do.

It is not a magical device.

It is not an end-all solution.

It is not a road map toward total success.

This manual only attempts to open a dialogue, begin or continue a discussion and help you think your way through the processes as you set a vision for your future.

This manual is only of help if you are willing to go through some of the suggested processes.

Best wishes.

Requests for additional information should be addressed to: virgilrevish@yahoo.com or pearre89@aol.com.

WHAT IS YOUR VISION?

Children are often asked: What do you want to be when you grow up? Sometimes children will have an answer and sometimes they will not. Yet families, without exception, generally want their children to succeed in school and life. Parents often have the vision that their children will have bright and shining careers. Sometimes that turns out to be their realities. Sometimes, unfortunately, it may not turn out that way at all. There are no guarantees but always there are steps that can be taken to give the "Visionary" an edge and even a beginning.

To make long term and future goals achievable, children must be encouraged from the beginning of their school years to value learning and to always do the best work possible. Additionally, they should be encouraged, by parents, teachers, and others, to participate in extra-curricular activities and sports. The student with a Vision should be well-rounded. Extra-curricular activities, reading programs, and positive relationships that offer encouragement, support, and even challenge may increase their exposure to many opportunities as well as provide firm foundations upon with the student's academic success will grow, gain momentum and help them to succeed.

Going back to the original question, "What do you want to be when you grow up?" the answers each student gives may vary from time to time as one gains more awareness of the possibilities. Yet, this should remain a vital consideration as a student grows throughout his/her academic life. For those who have named a profession, they should be introduced to the course of study that will help them gain the knowledge that will lead them to where they are determined to go.

Parents should be careful about setting the vision for the student. Students, through a variety of life experiences, will decide what they want to be or do. Again, this may change many times over the years as the student gains more experience. But in general, a great place to start is to ask your student:

What do you want to be when you grow up? This can and should often be followed by: what can we do to make that happen?

Regardless of the answer, the real question is about his or her ultimate goals. What does this student need to have a vision, a goal, or a dream? If they want to be a teacher, that is good. If they want to be a doctor, that is also good. If they want to be a fireman, police officer, or some other professional or even non-professional, let the student dream as long as they understand, it is their future. We, as adults and parents, are just a bit more experienced in helping them get to their next steps if we are aware, interested, and supportive.

But each child's future is best achieved when it starts with a student's dream, which we call VISION, and when that Vision is advanced through the processes and steps that are required to get them where they want to be.

THE ROLES PARENTS
MUST PLAY

P arents will always play critical roles in how their children grow, progress, and succeed. Training begins at home. Successful students tend to have similar commonalities. They are disciplined and creative. They are confident and excited about life. They respect authority. They listen and respond appropriately. They follow directions. They tend to be courteous and have a positive sense of self-worth.

Children must feel respected and appreciated. They must feel valued and worthy of praise from their family, teachers, friends, and others. These are just some of the attributes that help the student grow in positive directions. There are, however, other concerns that must be considered.

These include simple, yet necessary, considerations like appropriate bedtimes. Students need rest to be attentive and focused as they attempt the challenges of learning.

Students require, desire, and need cor-rection that is firm but caring. They need a loving insistence of excellence. These simple on-going influences at home may help guide and encourage students to be their best at school.

We encourage parents to know their children honestly and well and to appreciate and encourage their student's efforts to be "excellent." Parents, please set high but reasonable standards while realizing that children are not yet adults. They will make some mistakes as they grow but thankfully, they have parents who will guide them.

In all instances, however, there are some things and behaviors that must be practiced from a very young age. This includes saying, "Thank You" and "Please." Other behaviors must be addressed as the child grows. Never expect a 3-year old to be able to make the decisions that a 10 year must make. Be present with your child when you can and be always supportive of their attempts to be creative, athletic, or talented and skilled. Always telling a child to "sit down" or "be quiet" or "don't" or "you can't," may discourage a child from trying to develop his/her skill, talent, and natural ability. Of course, use good judgment but remember, children must be able to positively express themselves because they are growing. They are trying new things. You never know who your child can become.

DISCIPLINE

From a very young age, children need and expect discipline. Appropriate measures for appropriate and inappropriate behaviors must be practiced by parents as students grow and experience new environments, situations, and experiences. When children enter school, basic self-discipline is expected. Parents who allow children to "talk back" at home may expect that behavior at school and in other inappropriate places. Remember, teachers are challenged with the many challenges of educating. They cannot always stop to discipline children with inappropriate attitudes and behaviors. Having to do so not only disrupts the classroom and deprive other students of learning but also denies the constant offending student the opportunity to learn grown and achieve. While children should be encouraged to speak their thoughts and concerns, they should be taught what is appropriate and what is not.

Children can be confused by what parents expect and tolerate versus what schools tolerate and expect. Parents must be reasonable, rational, and able to make the decisions in the best interests of all. It has been said that what parents present in their private lives is what children learn. If children are exposed to violence, argumentative behaviors, and learn to live in fear that is what will govern their academic experience.

Children cannot always separate their environments at an early age. If they live in "unsafe" "loud" and "disruptive" environments and then come to school needing to be secure, focused, and preparing for their success often they cannot simply "forget" or put aside what they have experienced in the home. Throughout the day and underlying all that the student tries in school will filter through their thoughts, hurts, and fears as they attempt academic success. Too often, that just does not work in the student's best interest.

It is smart to think that just as children learn, so must parents learn what the acceptable, appropriate, and permissible behaviors are. Proper train-ing does and should start at home with the people students love, know, believe in, trust, and hope to please.

In helping the student to set goals and reach them, parents are encouraged to take realistic self-evaluations. Many times parents are doing the best they can. Sometimes they will benefit from taking parenting classes through social service agencies, YMCAs, churches, and other community-based initiatives. Many have been surprised to find how much support and information have helped to improve their relationships with their children and their images of themselves.

Parenting is critical to a child's development. Children will long remember and cherish or resent the relationships they have experienced in their lives. Be the kind of parent your student will appreciate your personal, loving, and supportive investments in his/her education and future.

SELF-DISCIPLINE AND BEHAVIOR

For young children, toddlers even, discipline is required. That is just a natural need. As a child grows, however, there can be tricky or even grey areas in the discussion of "discipline" versus "self-discipline." It is interesting sometimes to know that a child who has been allowed to "act anyway" at home, will come to school and adopt appropriate behaviors and meet those standards in school simply to be accepted. And sometimes just the opposite is true.

Have you ever been to the store or a restaurant, where a baby is crying without ceasing and parents go merrily along much to the irritation of others? What is that teaching the child? Have you seen toddlers allowed to scream without correction? Have you been to a doctor's office where children are allowed to run, romp, and interfere with the normal business of the office? Discipline is required. It is the parent's responsibility to provide his/her child with the tools that make them socially acceptable.

As a child grows, the decision-making process is expressed through a child's behavior. When told "No", how does the child react? Does the child have tantrums? Does the child know when to be quiet and when to speak? How does the child act when being corrected? Does the child pout, sulk, or otherwise show displeasure?

All the answers to all the questions raised have to do with the child's ability to know right from wrong and to act accordingly. Always it is the expectation that parents know and are attuned to right and wrong, to know and employ, rather than to ignore, appropriate disciplinary strategies and inappropriate, unacceptable behavior.

In the beginning for example in the early grades, students will be lead to sit, stand, and be quiet. As they grow, however, it is expected that they know and will comply. Can the child turn off bad behavior? Parents need to know and understand their children and to determine if they are engaged in helping the child to learn and achieve acceptable levels of achievement. No one can teach a child who is not emotionally developed and prepared to learn. If a parent sees the evidence that a child is uncontrollable, or has great lapses in judgment which negatively impacts his or her ability to learn, counseling or even medical intervention may be required. As children grow, they are expected to have acceptable levels of behaviors, performance, and social skills.

Can children learn self-discipline? Yes, they can! Again, however, sometimes, children's behaviors are reflections of what is allowed or happens and what is said and done at home. Parents need to understand the implications of their words and behaviors toward the child. The parent who calls a child stupid, fat, or other demeaning words will, most likely, develop low self-esteem problems that they may hide at home but will act out in school. They may become shy individuals afraid of failing; or often, afraid to succeed for fear of being noticed. Children who hear the constant inappropriate language at home may surely share what they know and have learned in the home and be subject to disciplinary actions. Children who experience domination and violence in the home may "act" as gentle and loving spirits at home but be loud-mouthed bullies in the larger community which is often the school.

Parents need to understand their roles in helping students to identify, set, and achieve their goals. They must understand how their behavior impacts the day and sets up a course for their lives. It is fair to say, successful and unsuccessful children become who they have learned to be.

Self-discipline does not mean you have a perfect child but a child who knows how to turn off the bad, negative behaviors, and how to control their emotions, good and bad. Self-discipline includes the ability to turn off the "noise" of life so that the student can read, focus, learn, and grow.

Parents must be attentive to and involved in their child's growth and development. For those who do not

11

know or who need to sharpen their parental skills, you are encouraged to do so at the earliest possible time in or before the child's arrival in the world and certainly as they grow. That requires honesty. We all learn to learn. Learning appropriate parenting is vital to a child's success as is the child's ability to know right from wrong, acceptable behavior, and the ability to make the right choices at the right time. This is because when the child is home, they are your responsibility. When they are in external environments, others expect them to be accountable and ready to mix, socially, emotionally, responsively, and educationally, with others in ways that are beneficial positively for all.

WHAT PARENTS CAN DO NOW

Once again, it is necessary to point out that the most important people in a child's life are, or should be the parents. Children, at the youngest ages, spend the greatest amounts of time at home. Parents will notice that when babies see you laugh, they laugh. Likewise, they feel your sadness, disappointment, hurt, and anger. They also feel your impatience and intolerance, though they may not understand it.

It trying to help your student learn, grow, and achieve, be involved. In being involved, bring positive, rather than consistent, harsh, critical, and judgmental energy into the learning/sharing experience. Even from an early age, your positive interaction may help in more ways than you can imagine.

Depending upon the age of your child, here are some things you may want to consider and try:

- Help your child begin positive learning experiences:
- Color, draw and do or oversee artwork/crafts with your child
- Play games, even educational games, with your child
- Read to Your Child
- Allow your child to read to you
- Check homework regularly
- Correct English/Grammar, Spelling in homework
- After a movie, story, or new experience: ask questions: What did you think? How did you feel?
- Encourage children to express their feelings appropriately without your judgment
- Limit television, video games, and cell phone usage.
- Attend their extra-curricular activities such as concerts (band and choir); athletic events
- Visit the school; talk with teachers, ask how you can help
- Play Positive Music: *I Believe I Can Fly* or *The Greatest Love of All*
- Introduce positive thoughts through poetry, prose, and Quotations:
- *Harlem (A Dream Deferred); Don't Quit*
- Remember this guidance:

Proverbs 22:6
Train up a child in the way he should go;
even when he is old he will not depart
from it.

For your convenience and consideration, the words to
these suggested (examples) of songs and poetry follow:

"I Believe I Can Fly" by **R. Kelly**

I used to think that I could not go on
And life was nothing but an awful song
But now I know the meaning of true love
I'm leaning on the everlasting arms

If I can see it, then I can do it
If I just believe it, there's nothing to it

[Chorus:]

I believe I can fly
I believe I can touch the sky
I think about it every night and day
Spread my wings and fly away
I believe I can soar
I see me running through that open door
I believe I can fly
I believe I can fly
I believe I can fly

See I was on the verge of breaking down
Sometimes silence can seem so loud
There are miracles in life I must achieve
But first I know it starts inside of me, oh

If I can see it, then I can be it
If I just believe it, there's nothing to it

[Chorus:]

Hey, cause I believe in me, oh

If I can see it, then I can do it (I can do it)
If I just believe it, there's nothing to it

[Chorus:]

Hey, if I just spread my wings
I can fly. I can fly. I can fly, hey
If I just spread my wings
I can fly-eye-eye-eye
Hum, fly-eye-eye

Greatest Love of All - Whitney Houston

I believe the children are our future
Teach them well and let them lead the way
Show them all the beauty they possess inside
Give them a sense of pride to make it easier
Let the children's laughter remind us how we used to be
Everybody searching for a hero

People need someone to look up to
I never found anyone who fulfilled my needs
A lonely place to be
So I learned to depend on me

[Chorus:]

I decided long ago, never to walk in anyone's shadow
If I fail, if I succeed
At least I live as I believe
No matter what they take from me
They can't take away my dignity
Because the greatest love of all
Is happening to me
I found the greatest love of all
Inside of me
The greatest love of all
Is easy to achieve
Learning to love yourself
It is the greatest love of all

I believe the children are our future
Teach them well and let them lead the way
Show them all the beauty they possess inside
Give them a sense of pride to make it easier
Let the children's laughter remind us how we used to be

[Chorus:]

I decided long ago, never to walk in anyone's shadow
If I fail, if I succeed

At least I live as I believe
No matter what they take from me
They can't take away my dignity
Because the greatest love of all
Is happening to me
I found the greatest love of all
Inside of me
The greatest love of all
Is easy to achieve
Learning to love yourself
It is the greatest love of all

And if by chance, that special place
That you've been dreaming of
Leads you to a lonely place
Find your strength in love **Harlem** by Langston Hughes
What happens to a dream deferred?

Does it dry up
like a raisin in the sun?
Or fester like a sore—
And then run?
Does it stink like rotten meat?
Or crust and sugar over—
like a syrupy sweet?
Maybe it just sags
like a heavy load.
Or does it explode?

Don't You Quit
Author Unknown

When things go wrong, as they sometimes will,
When the road you're trudging seems all uphill,
When the funds are low and the debts are high,
And you want to smile, but you have to sigh,
When care is pressing you down a bit-
Rest if you must, but don't you quit.
Life is queer with its twists and turns,
As every one of us sometimes learns,
And many a fellow turns about
When he might have won had he stuck it out.
Don't give up though the pace seems slow -
You may succeed with another blow.
Often the goal is nearer than
It seems to a faint and faltering man;
Often the struggler has given up
When he might have captured the victor's cup;
And he learned too late when the night came down,
How close he was to the golden crown.
Success is failure turned inside out -
The silver tint in the clouds of doubt,
And you never can tell how close you are,
It might be near when it seems afar;
So stick to the fight when you're hardest hit -
It's when things seem worst that you must not quit.

Perhaps the suggested songs and poems will lead parents, students, and mentors to other music and writings that will encourage students as they grow. These may, as well, be good topics for discussions with parents and their students. This is just a beginning. Learn to encourage yourself, your students, and others.

ACCOUNTABILITY AND RESPONSIBILITY

Being accountable and being responsible are attributes that children must learn even at an early age. Although we live in this technological age where things seem to happen at a very rapid pace, learning and living by standards will never change. It is easy to recognize that some things that used to take a long time to achieve happen within minutes or very short periods of. The internet, for example, gives us information that used to take days and long periods to research can now be received within minutes. Yet, the roadmap to long-term success still requires determination, patience, trial and error, and other attributes.

How does one become accountable and responsible?

Once again, it begins at home. Even young children can be required to put things back where they belong. Teach children to pick up toys.

As children grow, chores are responsibilities. Taking out the trash, washing dishes, cleaning up the bedroom, making up the bed teaches both account-ability and responsibilities.

Emphasizing the importance of telling the truth is essential. "I didn't know," or "I don't know how," are often just as an excuse. "It is not my fault," is another buy-in sometimes that is both unacceptable and untrue. Even if "it isn't his/her fault" that cannot be a constant excuse for not having standards met. If parents begin and continue to accept excuses, provide alternative answers in situations that require pre-determined and normal outcomes, parents are not helping students to live lives that will lead or help them to become accountable and responsible adults.

REWARDS AND PUNISHMENTS

For everything one does in life, there may be rewards, punishments, consequences, and challenges. At every step, you will be required to make good decisions.

As you grow, meet new people, make new friends, maintain peer relation-ships there will be opportunities for you to demonstrate your maturity, your wisdom, and even your ability to be unique and individual.

Never run away from your challenges. In every situation, from the way you decide to dress to the people you allow into your circle of friends, the language you use, whether or not you do your homework, study for tests and exam, respect authority, and in many other ways, your only responsibility will be to make the decisions that help you meet your goals. Your decisions and your actions will often determine whether or not you receive a reward, penalty, or consequence.

Your everyday actions will make you eligible or ineligible to continue to participate in many activities and roles which require responsible behavior.

You may come to understand, and you must, that your feelings do matter, but more important will be what you decide to do. Your behavior counts.

You must make good decisions. When in doubt, be sure to talk with someone you trust, whose value you respect, and who has your best interest in mind. But in the end, always as in the beginning, your challenge will be to think and make good decisions.

READING REALLY IS FUNDAMENTAL

There can never be too much emphasis put on reading. Almost all learn-ing, whether in school, traveling, driving, cooking, or playing a game on the computer…. your ability to read and understand is critical. Many times a student's success is directly related to his/her ability to read, understand, and respond.

As students go from grade to grade, reading challenges grow. If at any time a student finds discomfort in reading, he or she should seek guidance and reading help. There are many tools available.

CAN YOU SAY "HONOR ROLL?

E verybody is not expected to achieve the same degree of academic success. Yet all students should be encouraged to always do their best. Honor roll often brings reward, notice, and a feeling of success. Schools use Honor Roll as a means of appreciating, noticing, and encouraging students to continue to study, learn, grow, and succeed.

Even if a student, seldom or never make the Honor Roll, there are many other ways in which a student can receive positive reinforcement from the school, the family, and the community.

For the student who consistently makes the Honor Roll, that student is setting a foundation for the consideration of Academic Honor and Awards, even scholarships as they make their plans to head off to college.

For the student, including athletes planning to attend college, grade point average is important. Most 4 year colleges and universities have clearly defined entrance requirements. They will look for consistency in the student's work as well as growth in areas. For the athlete, the school may have a one-grade point average while there is also academic compliance the college athletes must meet.

In summary, once again, families need to oversee study habits, school attendance, participation, academic growth, and other requirements that will help the student achieve his/her VISION and to meet their personal and academic goals.

The importance of Perfect Attendance – When students are consistently attending school, they consistently have the opportunities to learn without interruption. The game of catch-up due to absence can be quite challenging. Even if a student is enrolled in Pre-K learning experiences, they should attend regularly and on time. As the student grows through the educational process, of course, it reasons that students will learn better if they are PRESENT.

HIGH SCHOOL COURSE REQUIREMENTS FOR COLLEGE ADMISSION

Every student who anticipates attending college must complete the core course required by most colleges and universities. Each student should discuss with his/her guidance counselor and stay abreast of course, selection to qualify for the colleges to which they are seeking admission.

While the admission standards may vary from one college to another, nearly all colleges and universities will require that applicants have satisfied a standard core curriculum. These core courses usually offered in high school should be a top priority for students interested in continuing their education at a four-year college. Even those colleges and universities which offer open admissions will have that expectation. Students may sometimes be admitted provisionally, if they have not satisfied some of the requirements. Those students will be advised or even placed in remedial courses to gain an appropriate educational background for college readiness.

In general, a typical high school core curriculum will require:

English –	4 years
Foreign Languages –	2-3 years
Math –	3 years
Science –	2-3 years
Social Studies (including History)	2-3 years

When a college calculates the Grade Point Average (GPA) for admission consideration, the college may place more emphasis on the core course average than on the entire transcript or record of academic completion. Grades for Physical Education, Music (including Band and Ensembles), and other non-core courses are not as useful for predicting a student's level of college readiness as the core courses are.

The core course requirements vary from state to state. Some schools may require a review of the entire high school record (transcript) that goes beyond the core.

The chart below shows the minimum course recommendations from a sampling of colleges which have very selective admissions requirements:

English –	4 years
Foreign Languages –	2 years
Math –	3 years
Science –	3 years
Social Studies (including History)	2 years

You should note that generally 20 academic units are required.

WHAT IS ACADEMIC MERIT?

Merit is easily described as "value that deserves respect and acknowledges." It is a "good quality or praiseworthy characteristic that someone has." Academic improvement on the way to academic excellence may be praise-worthy. Being at the top of the class is certainly MERIT. But merit can be achieved in a variety of ways. Merit is often criteria for honor societies and other kinds of awards that students can achieve through their educational and even extracurricular activities. Students should be encouraged to achieve, even to excellence.

Merit is also a descriptive used when scholarships are considered and awarded. Without regard to financial need, merit is a consideration many scholarships/organizations may consider when making their awards.

The Value of Extra-Curricular Attendance – In school and throughout a student's school attendance, as well as outside of school, students will have many opportunities for social growth, learning how to positively interact with others and the importance of participation in a variety of activities. Some students will love the experience of group settings; others will be more introverted and or individual. While team sports like volleyball, football, baseball, softball, and even cheerleading are great exercises, other sports like art clubs, tennis, bowling, chess clubs, and other types of activities provide challenges and enjoyment for students.

Students will learn to engage with others, to aim for goals, whether team or individual and learn how to win and lose. They, through extra-curricular activities, build social and personal relationships as well as form positive foundations from which students can greatly achieve.

HOW TO SELECT A COLLEGE?

T he well prepared high school graduate will have many colleges from which to choose to continue his/ her education. Beyond high school, there are trade and vocational schools, specialty schools, community colleges, 4-year colleges, and 4 -year universities.

Sometimes in families, college preferences are depending upon where other members of the families have continued their education. Still, today, however, among our students, the graduating student may be the first in his or her family to attend college. There may be colleges and universities which will be recommended. At other times, students will become introduced to colleges through programs, reading, other friends, and many other ways.

Of course, the major course of student matched with what the student's goals are should be the main point to consider. But there are other considerations too. Does the student want to live at home or on campus? Does the student want to live away from home? What does the college campus look like?

As the time draws near for the student to decide, he/she should seek counsel and advice from those who will have the information that will help to make the best decisions.

Of course, this is just a quick and general look at these options that will help to decide which is best for your particular needs. Take the time to consider your choices and educational options as you gain additional information.

JUNIOR AND HIGH SCHOOL GUIDANCE AND CAREER COUNSELORS

For most college-bound students, important decisions and outcomes start with academic planning. Students at the earliest possible time should establish good relationships with their Guidance Counselors. These professionally trained individuals are filled with and have access to a wealth of information that will help the student plan and succeed. With the Counselor, students and their parents should discuss all academic concerns including the course of study to be undertaken. As well, test-taking strategies, and the "what to do this year" discussions are important. Information is always the best route to success, even from year to year as the student progresses through junior and high school.

Counselors will also have information that will help the student gain knowledge and access about opportunities through camps, leadership programs, community service, academic placement, awards, and other things that will help the student develop and grow.

TESTING

Testing is an important criterion for which students must be prepared. Generally, college-bound students will take the following tests:

The Preliminary SAT/National Merit Scholarship Qualifying Test (PSAT/NMSQT)

SAT and/or ACT

This program starts with the student who plans to attend college. What a general thought. Each student must prepare not just for college attendance but for overall academic and future success. The earlier the Vision is understood and goals are outlined, the better prepared the student will be walking into his or her future. And so, it starts, for many with testing. Generally, the PSAT is the first step.

The Preliminary SAT/National Merit Scholarship Qualifying Test (PSAT/NMSQT, co-sponsored by the College Board and National Merit Scholarship Corporation (NMSC), is a standardized test that provides practice for the Scholastic Aptitude Test (SATO.) and provides a chance to enter the NMSC scholarship programs. The PSAT/NMSQT measures:

- Critical reading skills
- Math problem-solving skills
- Writing skills

These are the skills one should have acquired through years of education and life experience. In general, students should take these tests to learn their academic strengths and weaknesses and to identify other skills and the knowledge that will be needed for college success. Once completed and the results are received, along with the Guidance Counselor, the student can better focus a course of students that focuses on preparation in those specific areas that will improve their chances of academic success.

SCHOLASTIC APTITUDE TESTS (SATS)

To help the student prepare to take the SAT, he/she should learn the format of the test question. The student must be able to follow directions exactly as the directions are given. The student must be able to read the question and address only what is required.

The Achievement Tests (SAT and ACT) will generally test in four academic areas: English, Math, Reading, and Science. All tests are timed and require a student to meet the registration deadlines which are always available through the high school guidance counselor and on-line.

Upon receiving the SAT or ACT application instructions, the student will be asked: to which colleges/universities the scores should be sent. Once the scores are received by the students and the targeted institutions of higher learning, the student may begin to receive more information and requirements, even offers from colleges and universities. The first step is to prepare and then to take the tests.

Again, the student needs to have good relationships with his/ her guidance counselors. The test has a fee. If the student cannot afford to take the test, he/she may request a fee waiver. More information on this is available through the Test Center and the Guidance Counselor.

It is advantageous for the student to learn the testing options for each grade. Particularly, as it regards the SAT, the student who receives a score less than he/she desires may retake the tests. The highest score from each subject area will be recorded. This helps many students gain admission to the college/university he or she desires.

Students should not wait until the senior year of college to begin testing. However, if the student does wait, he or she should know the testing dates and sites. It will be important to arrive on time. One important thing to know is that the well-rested student is better prepared for overall performance and success. Before the test, get a good night's rest. Arise in time to have a meal before the test begin. Arrive in the testing site early enough to become comfortable in the testing environment and then.... DO YOUR BEST.

COLLEGE VISITS AND TOURS

I t is never too early for a student to begin to explore college options. They should be encouraged to research, visit, and tour the institutions of their interest. Many times, local churches, sororities, and fraternities as well as others will offer College Tours at little or no costs. Students and families need to learn, often through newspapers as well as through organizations themselves and guidance departments, which tours are being offered.

- How do you feel on the campus?
- What majors are offered?
- What is the tuition?
- Are scholarship offers available?
- Is on-campus housing available?

- What is the student: teacher ratio?
- What are the graduation rates for each year?

Those are just a few of the questions that should be addressed to help students and families make the most informed decisions.

THE ADMISSIONS'
PROCESS

The Admissions process may vary from one institution to another. All will require an application. Some will require that the application be submitted electronically. Some will require an essay; some will not.

Most colleges and universities will have an Application Fee, which may range in the amount. If the student does not have the appropriate fees, many colleges/universities will allow the student to apply for a fee waiver.

It may be helpful for the student to request an interview with an Admissions' Counselor for specific information. The most important thing is for the student to learn the admissions' requirements, and submit the required fees, transcripts, letters of recommendation from teachers, counselors, community leaders, and others when they are requested. Deadlines matter.

Additionally, students should know that some colleges and universities offer Early Admission that applies to specific dates. This will not be every institution, but for those that do…this is a very important consideration. Besides being in the best interest of the university, it is helpful for the student to know as early as possible what some of his/her options are.

In summary and in general, the admissions process may include:

- Completion of the Admissions Application and Fees
- Submission of the ACT or SAT testing Scores
- The High School Transcript

FINANCIAL AID

The costs of attending college will vary from one school to another. While tuition is one consideration, even after the school selection is complete, the family will need to consider the overall budget and needs. Costs which include books, meals (board), on-campus living (room fees); transportation to and from school; lab fees, etc. should all be considered. Therefore, a relationship with the Counselor in the Financial Aid Office of the selected school is a good and necessary resource.

First, however, not everyone understands some very basic facts about financial aid and how it can help. Financial aid can be grants, scholarships, loans, and monetary contributions to meet the costs of attending college. No matter the grade the student is in, it is always a good idea to help students find opportunities to participate in camps and volunteer programs. As they grow, these same programs and experiences may provide tuition assistance to be used when the time comes. When people and agencies are aware of the student's potential and ability sometimes financial assistance will be offered. Even agencies that do not have such programs may create them just to help and support.

As well, within every community, churches, civic and social organizations, and others offer scholarships. Research through the internet will unveil scholarships and awards. It takes just a bit of time. Many times the application process is very simple. Every year, millions of dollars are not awarded because no one applies. Therefore, families should conduct the research to identify scholarship opportunities before the times for college applications arise. It is true that "the early bird gets the worm."

THE COLLEGE FINANCIAL AID PROCESS

Financial aid includes grants, scholarships, loans, and fellowships as well as other types of awards. You should know the difference.

Grants, scholarships, and fellowships do not have to be repaid. Loans do! The wise and informed student and family will seek grants and scholarships, although loans may be needed.

Many times grants are made on a first-come, first-served basis and/or an as-need basis. Scholarships may be awarded on several factors including merit. Some grants and even scholarships are awarded based on religious affiliation, ethnic backgrounds, and other criteria. Essays may be required as well as recommendations. Research, research, research. Know the opportunities that are available to you.

Every college has a financial aid office located on campus. You may call, write, or visit to obtain the information you will need. In general, however, there is a very general process.

All persons who are interested in receiving ANY type of Financial Aid must complete a Free Application for Financial Student Aid Form. This can be completed online at http://www.fafsa.ed.gov/.

Federal student aid in some instances is awarded on a first-come, first-served basis so it is wise to know the expectations and requirements. The income of the parent(s) is a basic consideration, so families should file taxes according to established guidelines. Awards are made based on the year before the student's admission.

Financial aid is awarded based on the tax year previous to the year of enrollment. Students under the age of 21 are described as dependent students meaning they will apply based on the income of their parents. It is wise to complete the Financial Aid application as soon as the taxes are filed. On this application, just as with the Application for SATs, you will be able to identify the schools to which you wish to have financial aid processed.

Each school, based on your application, will send you a Financial Aid Award letter that lets you know how you have been awarded. If there is a deficiency, you will have time to seek other alternatives, apply for loans, or even work a while to make up the difference. Your Financial Aid Counselor will be able to advise you.

One additional consideration is that many institutions will require the completion of the institution's application for Financial Aid. Be sure to ask.

STUDENT ATHLETES

For the student-athletes, it is important to understand first that you are first a student and then an athlete. Everybody may dream about the professional arena, whether in football, basketball, soccer, or cheerleading. It does not matter, when it comes to school, the playing field is the same. To qualify to compete and participate, you will have to meet certain criteria to be eligible to play.

There is always a grade point average consideration. So, it is wise to develop and practice good study habits. Read and increase your vocabulary. Do your homework. Pass your tests. Study your assignments and then, practice and participate in the sports you have selected.

You will still have to take the same tests (PSAT, SAT, or ACT). You will still have to have an acceptable grade point average of 2.0, for most schools, to be eligible.

When you are approaching your junior and senior years of high school, you want to be particularly aware of what the academic compliance criteria are for the schools you have as your top choices. Speak regularly with your guidance counselors to make sure you are on the right course.

Additionally, to complement your academic experience and supplement your athletic history, you may need and/or enjoy additional opportunities that will boost you a level higher as you plan your future.

It may be helpful to attend summer and special athletic camps in your community and other places which will give you training, guidance, and athletic experiences. You may find it beneficial to research through a search engine such as website Google Combine & University Camps Listings.

Some successful athletes have attended at many as seven such camps from which valuable experience was gained. We encourage you to give this a try.

Of course, your coach is a valuable resource. He or she has completed high school, college and may have even been associated with professional athletics in some capacity. Get to know your coach. Let him or her knows your interests and find out how your coach can be a Most Valuable Resource as put your VISION into action.

CHECK LIST

The following is designed to remind you of some of the things you may need to do or consider. This is not a complete list but will be helpful as you continue to build upon your VISION.

- When do you need to register for the following tests?
- What are the testing dates?
- Where will you take the tests?
- Which test do you need to take: The PSAT/SAT/ACT?

"When should you take these exams?" Which tests are required?

PSAT:

SAT:

ACT:

What are your scores? _____

Would you like to increase that score? <u>Yes/no</u>

What personal test scores would you like to show to colleges?

- What are your three top college/university choices?
- When will you file the Free Application for Federal Student Aid?
- Have you contacted the college/university of your interest?
- Did you review admissions processes and requirements?
- Did you receive your Student Aid Report (SAR)?
- Did you sign and return the SAR? financial awards
- Do you need to re-take the SAT or ACT

COLLEGE CONTACTS

Some colleges still offer hard copy College Catalogs that present an overview and courses of study. Many of the colleges offer virtual on-line tours. Please begin to research the colleges of your interest. Most have an *.edu* site name. For example, for Virginia State University, you can access the site by www.vsu.edu.

Each site will list specific requirements for each area of interest. Another site that may be helpful is www.schoolsondemand.com.

SAMPLE LETTER

If you are planning to attend college, seeking a financial scholarship, or have other specific needs, you may need to write a letter of interest to a college, coach, or another individual. As a general guideline, letters should be short, professional, and clearly state your need. You can find a template online to address all your letter writing needs and you are encouraged to find a style that bests fits your needs. An example follows:

Date
Name
Street Address
City, State, Zip Code

Dear Coach,

I am _____, *a (classification) student– an athlete at (current high school) located in (city, state). I am (height, weight) and am of (age) years of age. My primary position is (offensive/defensive). I also play (list positions that you play).*

I am a hard worker, a winner, and a unique (athlete, musician, cheerleader, and/or drama student) dedicated to becoming the BEST TEAM PLAYER I can be. Off the field, I plan to become a role model and positive leader in our community.

I am interested in learning more about the (team sport, club, organization) program at (university).

If you would like to view some of my highlights, please go to youtube.com/ (rest of the domain name). I can be contacted at the above address, or by email at (email address).

I look forward to hearing from you in the future.

Sincerely,
Your Name

ATHLETIC /SPORTS CAMPS AND COMBINES

There are many opportunities for students and athletes to enhance their skills, improve their performance, and/or enjoy their extra-curricular interests. Please research. Google the subject of your interest and find out the location, dates, fees, and other particulars, including whether or not there are scholarships to support your attendance.

THE RESULTS FROM THE PROGRAM "VISION GOING TO THE NEXT LEVEL"

Darcell Whitaker

Darcell Whitaker, a graduate of Petersburg High School, is continuing his college career at Norfolk State University. His story is one of the interests because to achieve his goals, he had to learn many lessons, change some of his behavior and practices, and renew his commitment to academic success.

He did not realize until he entered high school, that although he was a good athlete with much potential, he could participate in high school sports because he did not meet the requirements. In summary, he needed a grade point average of 2.0 and he just did not have it.

Determined to make his dreams come true, with the help of his father, Roy, and his high school guidance counselor, Darcell devised a plan and worked hard and consistently to put that plan into effect.

What did he do? Darcell:

- improved his overall academic performance and improved his grade point average (G.P.A.) by changing his study habits.
- worked consistently with a tutor in the areas in which he was having problems
- continued to work to condition his body to be physically
- prepared, competitive, and able
- scheduled regular workouts with the football team when it was possible

- developed and incorporated a workout plan for offseason, so that he would be active throughout the year.

It took time, hard work, and commitment, but in time, he began to meet all of his goals. During high school, he also took advantage of football and sports camps. In each of those, he also set new standards which resulted in new achievements.

Rather than adopt the attitude of failure, he worked harder. Through camps, he met many new challenges and opportunities and was determined that his past was not his end. Rather, it was not too late for him to turn his low pre-high school performance into a brighter future.

Some of the programs, camps, and clinics he attended were: The Petersburg High School Junior Clinic (Petersburg, VA); NCU 100, East which was by invitation only; the Maryland Technique in Maryland; Charles Wilson football Camp, Norfolk, Virginia; the East Carolina University Football Camp (North Carolina), and the Elite 100 Camp in New Jersey.

Highlights in Darcell's story include that he was accepted in the NCU 100. That was great because to participate he had to be invited. During that camp, Darcelle was selected Most Valuable Player and as a result, was invited to attend the Elite 100 Camp which is held in New Jersey.

Darcell's story of success can be found on the website: www.VirginiaPreps.com. While Darcell considers attending many colleges and universities including Duke, East Carolina, Georgia Tech, and Hampton, he was recruited and enrolled at Norfolk State University after overcoming all of his academic challenges.

Hard work, dedication, and commitment to his Vision worked for Darcell Whitaker and those characteristics can work for you as well.

Good luck.

CONCLUSION

The reason I wrote this Manual was a God-given opportunity. The Greek word for an opportunity as it appears in the Scriptures is Kairos. It means "favorable opportunity." Its derivatives imply "the right moment; that which lasts only for a while.

Kairos means a God-given opportunity is being offered to mankind at a specific moment in time. However, the word also implies that there is a risk – a risk of faith.

In other words, as time moves on, the opportunity can be missed. That is why we have to recognize our opportunities and we have to know our moment which lasts only for a while.

Writing this Manual made me a better man. In the daily course of human events, unique opportunities Kairous—to change the destiny of a person or a people appeal…exist for a moment. The test of that person or people is whether they will recognize it and respond in obedience to the One who is offering it, trusting in His ability to work to refrain from the opportunity God had for me.

I have information in the Manual that will work for any individual who applies him/herself to the process. It will work to help prepare you to receive college entrance, a scholarship, or entry into the sports collegiate program of your choice.

For the program to work in any household, you must have a team. The team must consist of the parent, student, guidance counselor, teachers, and coaches.

In summary, the time the student reaches the 9th grade, he/she must have a 2.0 or better grade point average. This is the foundation of your life. By the 11th grade, the student should have completed all the SOL test requirements. Having done so, the student should be situated to do well on the SAT and/or ACT tests. Athletes must also pass the Clearing House Standards.

If any additional information is needed, students and parents should not hesitate to call or visit the office of the Guidance Counselor, financial aid or admissions counselor, or contact me if I may be of help.

Good luck as you continue to define the path that will lead you to reach your Vision.

ABOUT THE AUTHOR:

Biographical Statement

Born May 15, 1951, to Willie and Viola Revish, I attended Virginia Avenue Elementary and A.P. Hill Elementary School. A 1970 graduate of Peabody High School. I attended John Tyler Community College and in 1975, I transferred to Virginia State College (University) where I also became a member of the ETA chapter of Iota Phi Theta Fraternity, Incorporated.

After leaving Virginia State College, I taught school at Peabody Junior High until I joined the United States Army where I served for 3/5 years after which, because of my devotion to students and education I taught school in Fairfax, VA for four years. Later, I worked at Petersburg Wastewater Treatment Plant, my job was testing water samples and read meters.

In 2003, I married Katie B. Harris and on July 21, 1989, our son, Pearre Donta Revish was born. Now a student majoring in psychology and mass communication at John Tyler Community College, he celebrated a Spring 2012, graduation and is currently enrolled at Virginia State University.

From September 1993 to June 1999, I started a volunteer program in six Petersburg School s called "School Watch". This program monitors the hallways and cafeteria, helps in the classrooms, and works at school activities. With more than 100 volunteers serving, the Program received local news (Channel 8) coverage and was recognized by letters of commendation from President Bill Clinton and Virginia Governor Gilmore.

In 2000, I worked in the after-school tutoring program, at the Children's Home of Virginia Baptist, called Achievers Plus. The program was three days a week and provided children with homework help, an afternoon snack, and after-school activities.

Continuing to pursue opportunities to serve students and the community, I volunteered with the Matoaca High

School football team and have now worked with the youth for over 35 years.

As a member of Third Baptist Church, Petersburg Virginia, under the Pastoral leadership of Reverend Leroy Cherry, I serve or have served as a deacon, Sunday and Vacation Bible School teacher, and van driver.

Now, in 2013 as I continue my commitment to youth, education, and our community, I began to work with other visionaries and committed community leaders to encourage our youth. We recently launched the "Pull Your Pants Up" project and video, of which I am an associate producer. This is a nation-wide initiative designed to encourage our youth to be responsible, accountable, and prepared to meet and exceed the acceptable societal standards and to rise above the norm. For more information, please view the video at www.pypu.net.

OTHER CONTRIBUTORS

The his Manual is made possible by the help and input of individuals who have a demonstrated devotion to helping students set and reach their goals. They include:

Berdenia Mason Kelley

A Career Specialist at Petersburg High School, Berdenia Mason Kelly teaches in the Jobs for Virginia Graduates program. She helps high school seniors learn the skills and prepare to enter the workforce. She encourages students to continue their education and works to help them achieve success.

Larry Brown

With more than 35 years as an educator and Entertainment Executive Director, Larry Brown holds both the B.S. degree and M.Ed (1995) from Virginia State University. Currently, he serves as chair of the SPED Department and EFE Coordinator with the Petersburg Public Schools. Among his accomplishments, Mr. Brown works with the National Focus on Success (Pull Your Pants Up) Project. He has earned the Black Belt in Karate and was Educator of the Year in 1997, co-founder of the School Watch Volunteer Program at Petersburg, High School (1997).

www.ingramcontent.com/pod-product-compliance
Lightning Source LLC
Chambersburg PA
CBHW052120030426
42335CB00025B/3073